Everything grows with love

Everything grows with Love

Irene Smit and Astrid van der Hulst

WORKMAN PUBLISHING · NEW YORK

Library of Congress Cataloging-in-Publication Data is available.
ISBN: 978-1-5235-0114-4

Cover art by Carolyn Gavin
Design by Lisa Hollander
Special thanks to Marjolijn Polman at *Flow* for managing this project.

Workman books are available at special discounts when purchased in bulk for premiums and
sales promotions as well as for fund-raising or educational use. Special editions or book
excerpts can also be created to specification. For details, contact the Special Sales Director
at the address below, or send an email to specialmarkets@workman.com.

Workman Publishing Co., Inc.
225 Varick Street
New York, NY 10014-4381
workman.com
flowmagazine.com

FLOW® is a registered trademark of Sanoma Media Netherlands B.V.
WORKMAN is a registered trademark of Workman Publishing Co., Inc.

Printed in China
First printing November 2017

10 9 8 7 6 5 4 3 2 1

Oh, how we love quotes and sayings—especially when they are about love.

We don't mean strictly romantic love—the word encompasses so much more than that. Love can be found anywhere, from a neighbor's friendly smile, to a sloppy kiss from a dear pet, to a hug from a family member, to being kind to yourself and others—*everything grows with love*.

Sometimes we want to share these feelings with those who have affected us most, but we can't seem to find the right words. In this book, you'll find page after page of musings on love—in all of its iterations—illustrated by our favorite artists. Naturally, we each have a favorite. Irene's is: "Never give up on the things that make you smile." This reminds her to always keep making time to do the things that make her happy with her loved ones, no matter how busy she may be. And Astrid's favorite is: "Happiness isn't a fixed point, it's always in a flux," because it's a good reminder that, in love and in daily life, after a dark day there's always a bright one on its way.

Savor the tiny moments, revel in the big ones, and appreciate the special people around you.

Irene & Astrid

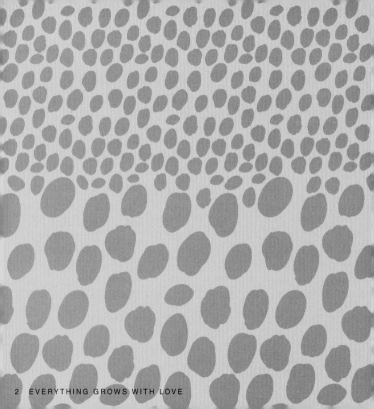

cooking for
my family.

WHAT IS DONE
IN LOVE
IS DONE WELL.

Small dreams.
Ideas. Words.
can manifest into
your greatest reality.

FROM

L I T T L E

T H I N G S

B I G

T H I N G S

G R O W

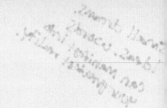

6 EVERYTHING GROWS WITH LOVE

THERE ARE *some things*
THAT WILL ALWAYS BE
imperfect

may your search
through nature
lead you to yourself

BE SOMEONE WHO MAKES SOMEONE ELSE LOOK FORWARD TO TOMORROW

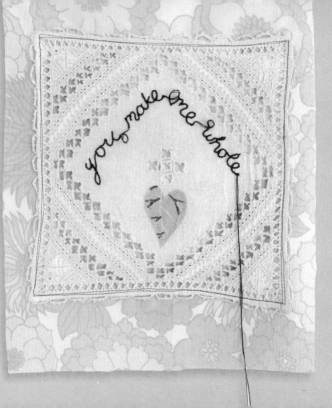

i love you to the moon and back

Always try
to be
a little kinder
than is
necessary

—J.M. BARRIE

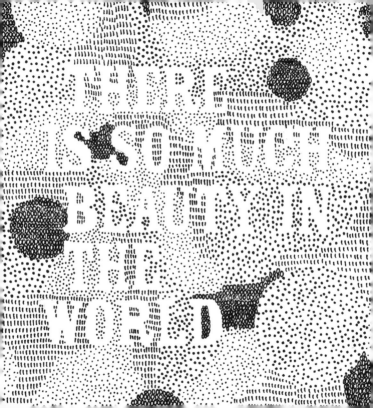

IT'S BETTER
FOR THE
heart
TO BREAK
than not to
BREAK

MARY OLIVER

Whatever our souls are made of,
his and mine are the same.

—EMILY BRONTË

YOU ARE *beautiful* INSIDE & OUT

TREAT ANYTHING YOU DO AS IF YOU'RE CREATING A PIECE OF ART

STAY HUNGRY STAY FOOLISH

♥

KINDNESS

IS THE

NEW

BLACK

Let's find a beautiful place
and get lost.

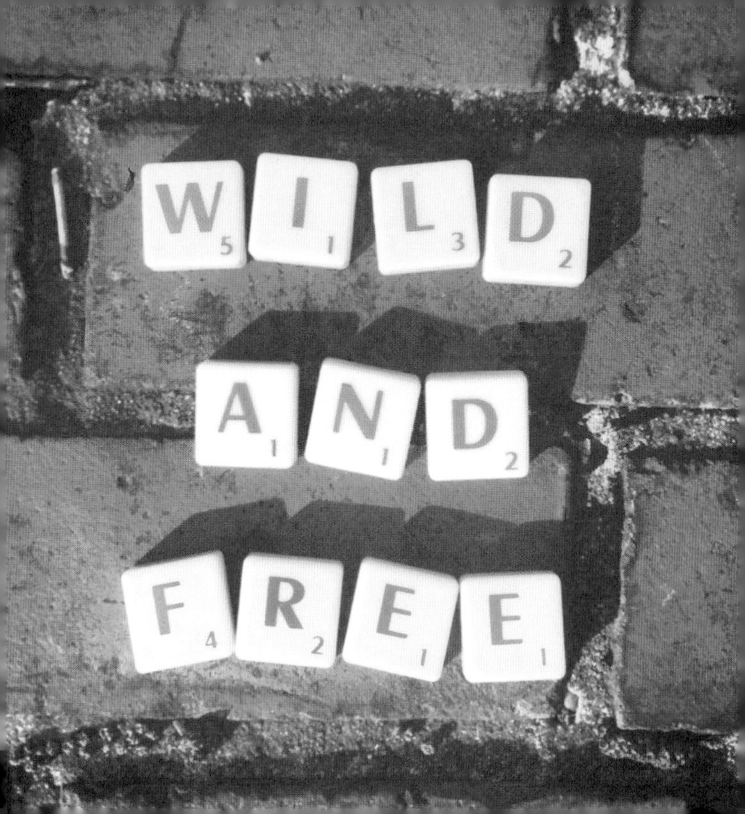
WILD
AND
FREE

THE SECRET TO A SUCCESSFUL RELATIONSHIP is PLENTY OF: JOY, curiosity, Passion & FUN

the smallest
things warm the ♥

YOU ARE MY SUNSHINE

come

nEST

with me

may our LOVE be forever LIKE pretty daisy chains. May NO PETALs FALL OR NO links Break AND MAY it feel natural & Beautiful ALWAYS.

"Wherever YOU go, YOU there are

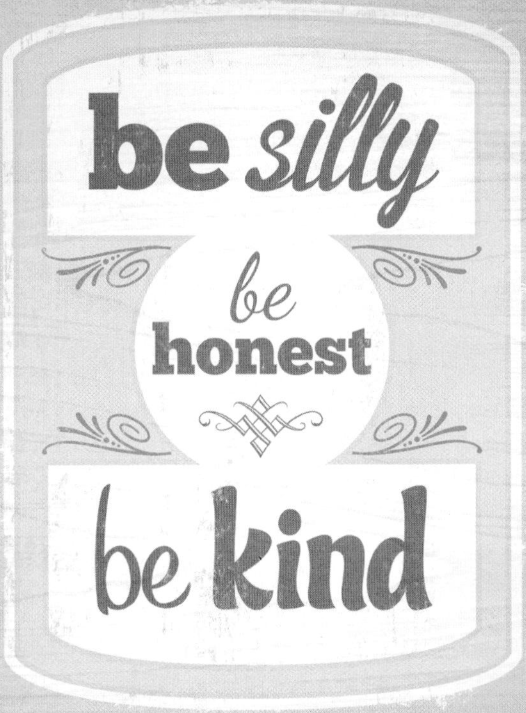
be silly
be
honest
be kind

I *think*
WE'RE
PRETTY
AWESOME
TOGETHER

♥

Dream with the STARS Smile WITH THE Sun

HOORAY,
IT IS
TODAY!

There's

NO PLACE LIKE

home

LOVE LIVES

HERE

IF NOTHING EVER CHANGED THERE WOULD BE NO BUTTERFLIES

YOU CARRY
SO MUCH
LOVE
IN YOUR HEART.
GIVE SOME
TO
YOURSELF.

I love what I do & MAYBE YOU WILL too

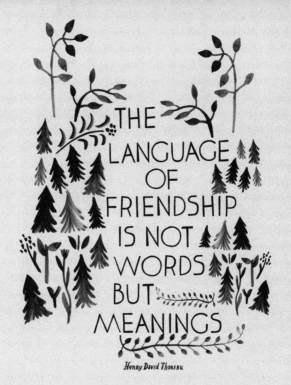

THE LANGUAGE OF FRIENDSHIP IS NOT WORDS BUT MEANINGS

Henry David Thoreau

Variety's the very spice of life,
That gives it all its flavor.

—WILLIAM COWPER

I CARRY YOUR HEART IN MY HEART

—E. E. CUMMINGS

EVERYTHING WILL BE OKAY IN THE END. IF IT'S NOT okay IT'S NOT THE end.

Create a
nice moment
for yourself

At least once a day

keep your face always
toward the sunshine
and the shadows will
fall behind you.

Live the life you love.

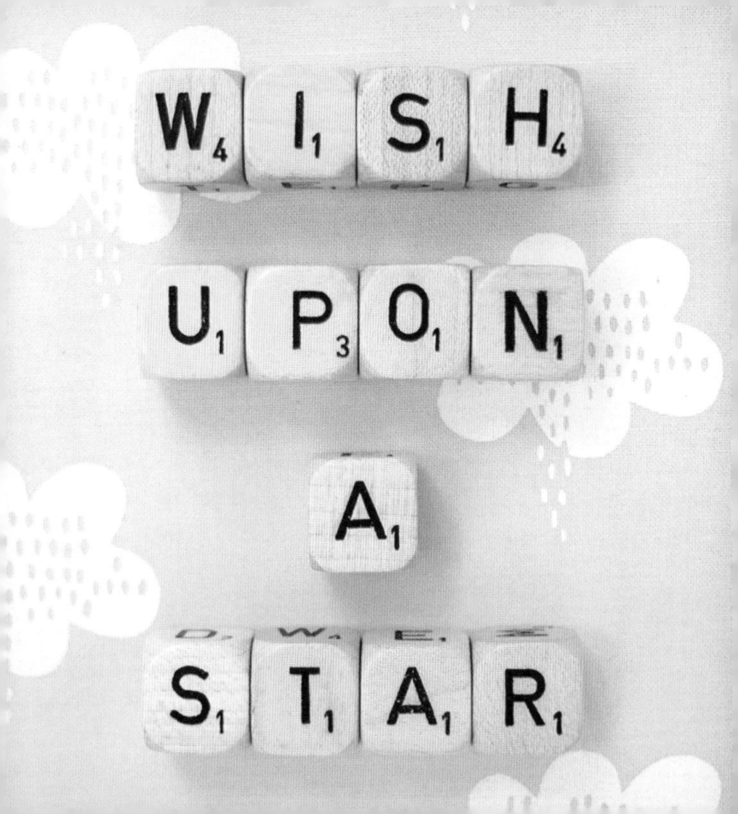
WISH
UPON
A
STAR

happiness is a FORM OF COURage.

GEORGE HOLBROOK JACKSON

HOLY MOLY
me
OH MY
YOU'RE
SUCH A
CUTIE PIE

The question is not what you look at, but what you see.

—HENRY DAVID THOREAU

I LIKE YOU

true friendship is when **friends** can walk in opposite directions and yet **remain** side by side.

THERE IS A
LOT OF
beauty
IN
ORDINARY
THINGS

Start EACH **DAY** with a happy LAUGH

I LOVE YOU
A BUSHEL AND A PECK
A BUSHEL AND A PECK
AND A HUG
AROUND THE NECK

IT FEELS GOOD
TO BE LOST IN
THE RIGHT
DIRECTION.

go confidently in the direction of your dreams

NOTHING YOU
RESOLVE TO DO
WILL MAKE YOU
MORE WORTHY
OF LOVE.
YOU ARE ENOUGH
RIGHT NOW.

CHOOSE HAPPINESS

i am thinking
nice thoughts
today

Holding you, I hold every thing.

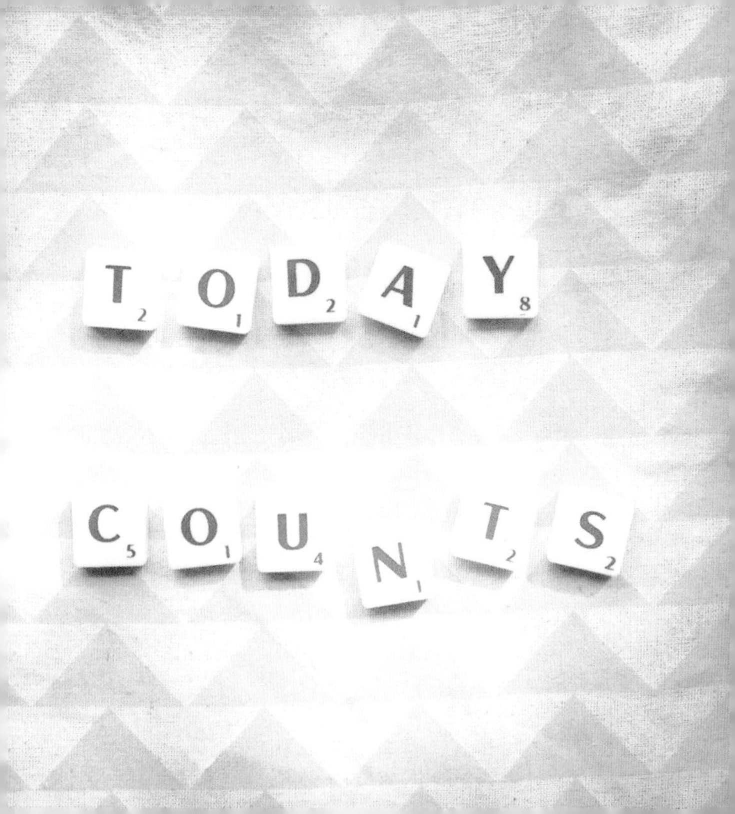
TODAY
COUNTS

Being able TO LAUGH ABOUT each other's ANNOYING HABITS is crucial

YOU'VE GOT A FRIEND IN ME

I'VE LOVED THE STARS TOO FONDLY TO BE FEARFUL OF THE NIGHT

Take the
unknown
and embrace
it like your
own

The Sea,
Once it casts its spell,
holds one in its net of
Wonder
Forever

It is one of the blessings of old friends that you can afford to be STUPID with them

Ralph Waldo Emerson

I love the Simple & tiny Things

Everything you can imagine is Real

Picasso

When you stop expecting
people to be perfect,
you can like them for who they are.

-Donald Miller

YOU
ME
→
YES
PLEASE

HERE
AND
NOW

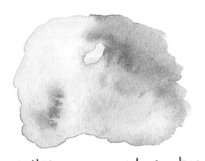

Great things are done by a
series of small things
brought together.
—Vincent Van Gogh

you are PEACHY perfect to me

dottie angel

WRAP AROUND ME LIKE my FAVORITE COZY SCARF protect me FROM the Chilly WEATHER + STAY CLOSE FOREVER ♥

IT'S NOT
WHERE YOU
LIVE
BUT
WHERE
YOU
LOVE

LIVE YOUR DREAM

Beauty

IS IN THE

Ordinary

-DIRK DE WACHTER

JUST WHEN THE
CATERPILLAR
THOUGHT THE WORLD WAS OVER
IT BECAME A BUTTERFLY

LOVE HAS NO UTTERMOST

as the STARS have no NUMBER

AND THE Sea NO REST

eleanor farjeon

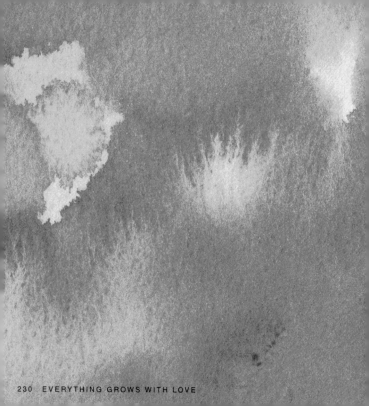

I knew
when I met you
AN
ADVENTURE
Was about
to happen.

ENJOY

the small

THINGS

TAKE ME

TO THE

SEA

IT SEEMS THEY HAD ALWAYS BEEN, AND WOULD ALWAYS BE, FRIENDS. TIME COULD CHANGE MUCH, BUT NOT THAT.

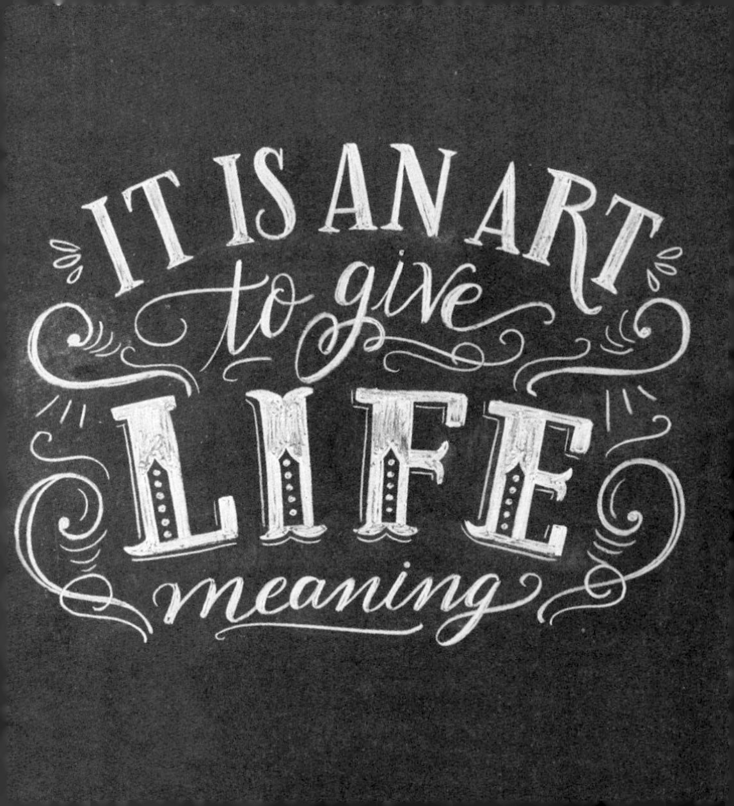

IT IS AN ART
to give
LIFE
meaning

Love
it will not betray you
dismay or enslave you,
it will
set you free —MUMFORD & SONS

YOUR
GREATNESS
IS NOT WHAT YOU
HAVE,
IT'S WHAT YOU
GIVE.

MAKE LIFE RICH LIKE CHOCOLATE CAKE

will you please

LOVE
ME

forever and a day

dottie angel

Collect moments, not things.

always do WHAT YOU aRE AFRAID TO do.

RaLpH WALDO EMERSON

the *best* things *come* *in* small *packages*

THINGS *are* *never* QUITE AS SCARY

when YOU'VE GOT *a* BEST FRIEND

BILL WATTERSON (CALVIN & HOBBES)

TODAY IS A PERFECT DAY to start LIVING YOUR DREAMS.

FRIENDSHIP IS A SIMPLE THING, AND YET COMPLICATED; FRIENDSHIP IS ON THE SURFACE, SOMETHING NATURAL, SOMETHING TAKEN FOR GRANTED, AND YET UNDERNEATH ONE COULD FIND WORLDS. —JAMAICA KINCAID

BE A LIGHT TO THE WORLD

live a little
love a lot

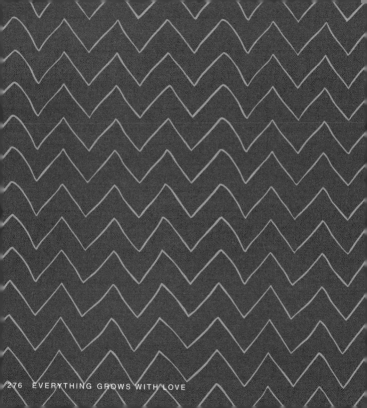

I AM GOING TO MAKE EVERYTHING AROUND ME BEAUTIFUL — THAT WILL BE MY LIFE.

'CAUSE YOU'RE

AMAZING

JUST THE

way

YOU ARE

- - - - - - -

Bruno
Mars

♥

Seize the DAY

— HORACE

YOU

- ARE my HAPPY -

Being somewhere is more important than **getting** somewhere

Michael Carroll

YOU PUT *the* BOOM BOOM INTO MY HEART

Document the moments you feel
most in love with yourself—
what you're wearing,
who you're around,
what you're doing.
Recreate and
repeat. —WARSAN SHIRE

Happiness isn't a Fixed Point it's always in Flux

a good life
is when you
smile often, dream
BIG, laugh a lot
& realize how
blessed you are
for what
you have

BE LIEVE IN YOURSELF

the MUSIC
IS NOT IN
the notes,
BUT THE
SILENCE
in between

—WOLFGANG AMADEUS MOZART

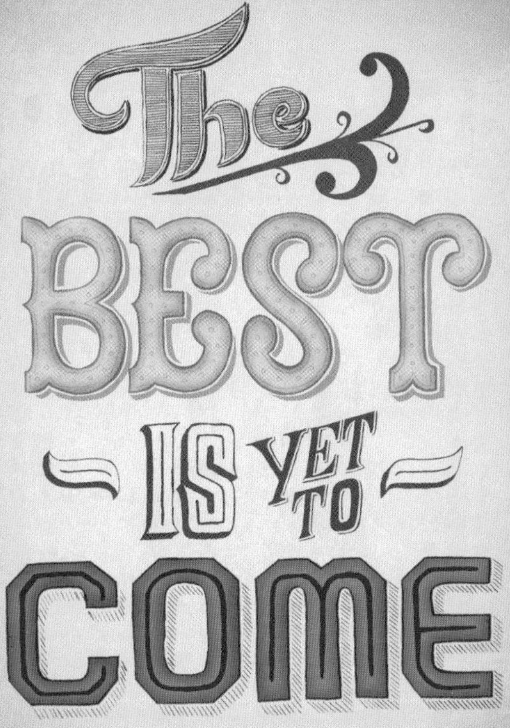
The
BEST
IS YET TO
COME

THE

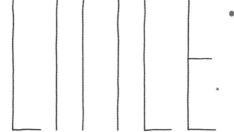

THINGS

Throw your dream into space like a kite,

and you do not know what it will bring back,

a new life, a new friend, a new love,

a new country.

—ANAÏS NIN

it's a beautiful
WORLD

EXPERIENCES BRING US Closer TO other people

You can't sleep? Me neither.
Let's can't sleep together.

The Future BELONGS TO THOSE WHO BELIEVE IN THE BEAUTY OF THEIR Dreams

There ARE BETTER

things ahead

than any we

LEAVE Behind

— C.S. LEWIS

FIND A PATH BEFORE A PATH FINDS YOU

Shine
LIKE A
PENNY
and
give
LOVE
BY THE POUND

Be
ALWAYS
BLOOMING

There are all kinds of love in the world,
but never the same love twice.

—F. SCOTT FITZGERALD

TREAT YOURSELF AS YOU WOULD TREAT A GOOD FRIEND

KRISTIN NEFF

SHARE YOUR ♥ LOVE ♥

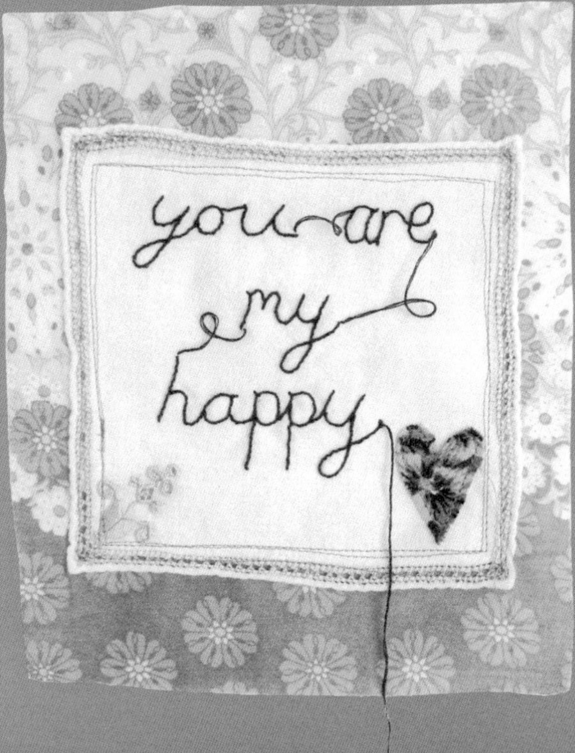
you are
my
happy

Someone
HOLD THE
sunlight
BACK 'CAUSE
we want this
NIGHT to last

—Wilkinson

BE FILLED WITH JOY

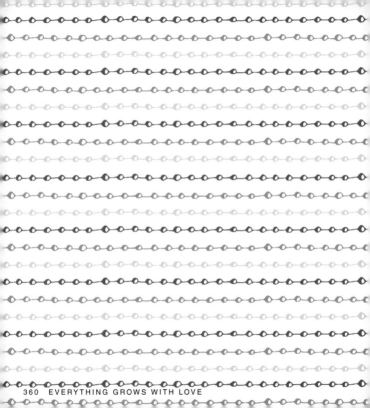

You're just what I needed

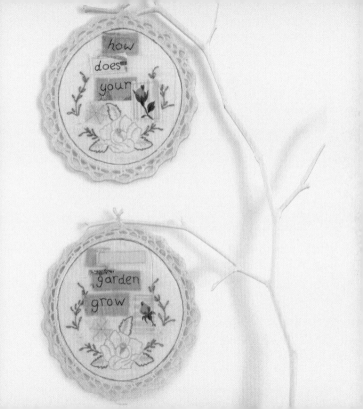

Keep some room in your heart

for the unimaginable.

—Mary Oliver

IT ALL COMES DOWN
to being able
TO
WAIT

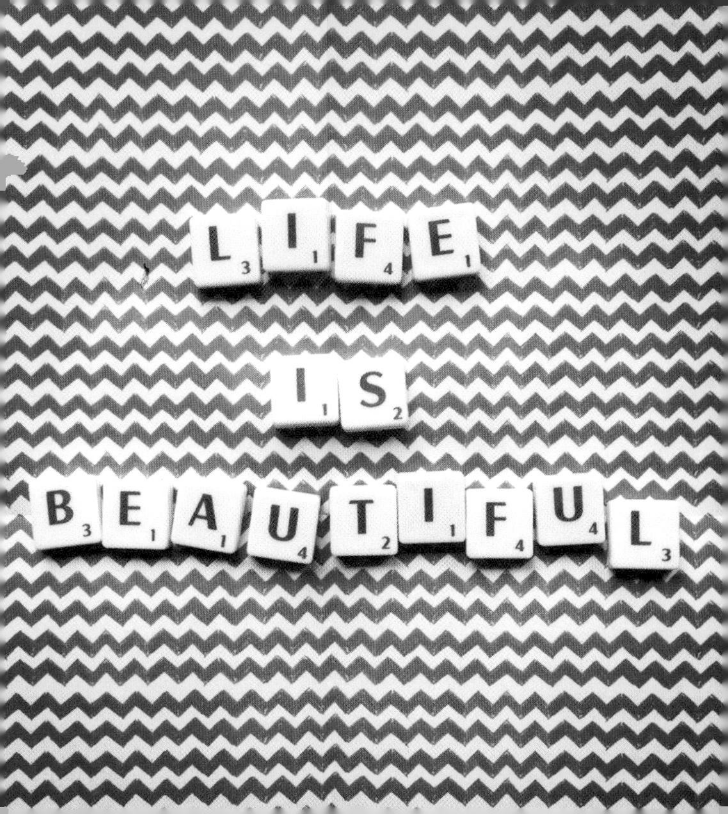
LIFE
IS
BEAUTIFUL

LOVE WHAT YOU CREATE

Never give up on the things that make you smile

KEEP having ADVENTURES together

— JOHN GOTTMAN

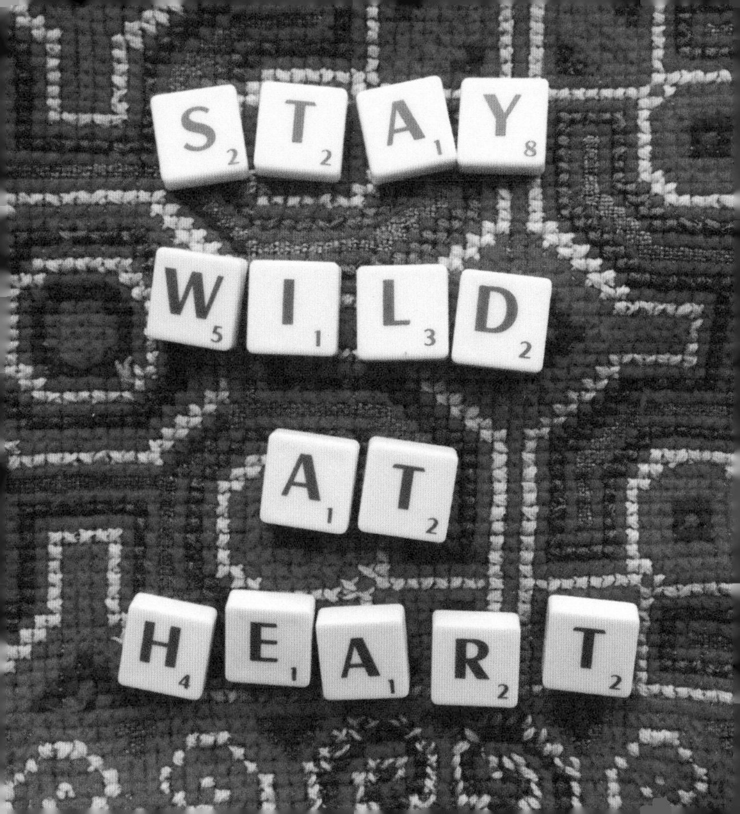
STAY
WILD
AT
HEART

You are the best mother, father, sister, friend, cousin, and lover you will ever have. —Oprah Winfrey

The best thing
to hold on to in life
is each other

THE ONLY
SOLUTION
IS
LOVE

Credits by Artist

AIKO FUKAWA: pages 47, 79, 103, 129, 147, 169, 195, 215, 239, 257, 269, 299, 323, 345, 363, 373, 389; **ANDREA D'AGUINO:** pages 33, 333; **ASTRID VAN DER HULST:** pages 9, 31, 49, 89, 111, 131, 151, 171, 199, 217, 237, 271, 291, 303, 325, 347, 359, 377, 387; **CAROLYN GAVIN:** pages 65, 125, 191, 259, 287, 385; **CHERYL RAWLINGS:** pages 21, 45, 59, 77, 123, 163, 181, 209, 229, 251, 285, 313, 341, 357; **DEBORAH VAN DER SCHAAF:** pages 23, 61, 91, 109, 185, 231, 265, 295, 349, 391; **DOTTIE ANGEL:** pages 19, 57, 121, 161, 207, 227, 255, 315, 355, 371; **JAMES WILLIAMSON:** pages 10,12,14,28,32,102,116,122,128,148,154,164,180,188, 208,228,232,266,272,312,320,332,334,388; **JANS ONTWERPFABRIEK:** pages 85, 97, 141, 189, 235, 293, 317, 337; **LISA HOLLANDER:** pages 267, 379; **MABLE TAN/ HAPPEE MONKEY:** pages 5, 41, 55, 73, 119, 143, 159, 179, 205, 225, 247, 277, 309, 331, 365; **MARLOES DE VRIES:** pages 13, 29, 107, 223, 307; **MEGAN NICOLAY:** pages 83, 139, 175, 241, 283, 311, 351; **NICOLE MIYUKI SANTO/GROUNDED ON THE DAILY:** pages 15, 37, 53, 71, 91, 115, 133, 155, 177, 203, 221, 245, 275, 305, 327; **OH SO PRETTY PARTY:** pages 27, 67, 101, 127, 149, 167, 197, 263, 297, 321, 343; **M.J. KOCOVSKI/PARS CAELI:** pages 3, 17, 43, 93, 117, 135, 157, 249, 279, 393; **SARAH TRUMBAUER:** pages 7, 75, 95, 137, 183, 253, 289, 335, 369; **VALERIE MCKEEHAN:** pages 35, 51, 69, 113, 153, 173, 219, 243, 301, 329, 353, 361, 375, 383; **VALESCA VAN WAVEREN:** pages 25, 213, 381; **VIKTOR CHALKBOARD:** pages 11, 39, 201, 273; **WICKED PAPER:** pages 63, 81, 87, 105, 145, 165, 187, 193, 211, 233, 261, 281, 319, 339, 367

Additional credits:
ADOBE STOCK: pages 104, 144, 168, 232, 386; **DREAMSTIME:** pages 2, 34, 50, 58, 80, 96, 132, 140, 152, 196,234, 244, 256, 260, 264, 274, 280, 342, 352, 360, 372, 379; **SHUTTERSTOCK.COM:** pages 8, 30, 40, 54, 66, 78, 98, 106, 112, 130, 170, 172, 184, 210, 214, 224, 242, 248, 276, 292, 300, 302, 322, 336, 340, 352, 356, 362–364, 380

Source Notes

PAGE 3: "What is done in love is done well" is a line slightly adapted from a letter Vincent van Gogh wrote to his brother, Theo, published in *Dear Theo: The Autobiography of Vincent Van Gogh*. **PAGE 71:** "Somewhere Over the Rainbow" is the title of a song written by Yip Harburg (1896–1981) with music by Harold Arlen (1905–1986) for the movie *The Wizard of Oz*. **PAGE 145:** "I love you a bushel and a peck" is a lyric from the song "A Bushel and a Peck," written by Frank Loesser (1910–1969). **PAGE 175:** "You've Got a Friend in Me" is the title of a song written Randy Newman for the movie *Toy Story*. **PAGE 177:** "I have loved the stars too fondly to be fearful of the night" is a line from the poem "The Old Astronomer" by Sarah Williams (1837–1868). **PAGE 193:** "You are my sun my moon and all my stars" is excerpted from the poem "38" by E. E. Cummings (1894–1962). **PAGE 231:** The line is inspired by *Winnie the Pooh* by A. A. Milne. **PAGE 239:** The line is inspired by *Winnie the Pooh* by A. A. Milne. **PAGE 253:** "Let us lay in the sun . . ." is from a song by Neutral Milk Hotel. **PAGE 275:** "Live a little love a lot" is from a song by David Lee Murphy and Shane Minor, performed by Kenny Chesney. **PAGE 297:** "You put the boom boom into my heart" is a lyric from the song "Wake Me Up Before You Go-Go," written by George Michael. **PAGE 393:** "The only solution is love" is from Dorothy Day's autobiography, *The Long Loneliness*.

About the Authors

Irene Smit and Astrid van der Hulst are the founders and creative directors of *Flow* magazine, a popular international publication packed with paper goodies and beautiful illustrations that celebrate creativity, imperfection, and life's little pleasures. Astrid and Irene began their careers as editors at *Cosmopolitan* and *Marie Claire*. In 2008, inspired by their passion for paper and quest for mindfulness, Irene and Astrid dreamed up the idea for their own magazine in a small attic and haven't looked back since. They live with their families in Haarlem, Netherlands.